Under
Construction

Under Construction

Developing Godly Character

Tony Sheard

Living Word UK

Under Construction: Developing Godly Character
Copyright © 2020 Tony Sheard
First Edition, ~September 2020

ISBN 9798679943759

Copyright Acknowledgements

Thanks

I want to give thanks to my wife Julie for all her support during the making of this book. She has always been the essence of godly character and I have learned much from her.

I also want to thank all my ministry Trustees for their help and support.

Special thanks goes to my good friend and fellow minister, Robin Henderson, who has faithfully proofed, edited and generally provided many suggestions that have improved the final result of this book. I am indebted to him.

Contents

Foreword

I'm thrilled to have this opportunity to commend this excellent book by Tony Sheard.

Those who know Tony will be delighted to hear that what he has written bears all the marks of the thoroughness and thoughtfulness that we have come to expect and enjoy from his ministry.

If, however, you are new to Tony's ministry, this book will provide an excellent introduction to Tony's coaching skills. I cannot think of anyone better to recommend to those wanting to develop a godly and mature character than Tony.

It is a sad fact that many today think that ministry is more about anointing than about character. Nothing could be further from the truth. When the Apostle John wrote, in his first letter, of us having an anointing that teaches us all things, I'm sure that one of the things that the anointing of which he wrote has come to teach us is the importance of godly character. How will people take notice of what we say if who we are is proving too great a distraction?

I can assure you that no matter how far you have come on your spiritual journey, this book will help to take you forward. It provides an excellent guide, steering you through scripture and offering plenty of practical advice.

I know that you will be glad that you have read this book and I'm sure that through your life it will also speak to those around you.

Dr Hugh Osgood
Founder and President of CIC International

Introduction

When something is under construction, particularly a building, it is obvious that change is taking place. Most people will follow the progress with anticipation over the final result. At that stage they know it is not finished, but equally they know that, provided there are no problems on the way, eventually it will be and they can admire the final result. That is the purpose of this book in relation to developing godly character. With regard to that I first want you to consider character in relation to Job.

Job is often commended for his patience but, on three occasions, God praises Job for his character (Job 1:1; 1:8; 2:3). The character traits identified in these three short testimonials are almost identical: blameless; upright; God-fearing; shuns evil; and integrity under pressure.

> *Then the LORD said to Satan, "Have you considered My servant Job, that there is none like him on the earth, a blameless and upright man, one who fears God and shuns evil? And still he holds fast to his integrity, although you incited Me against him, to destroy him without cause."*

Job 2:3

God clearly delights in Job and in his character. To put it in contemporary language, God was exercising His 'bragging rights'. Job did not understand everything about God, but he knew enough for it to affect the way he lived his life.

It was Job's character which enabled him to persevere through this adversity. So, would you like to have a character like Job's? Think about God exercising his bragging rights over you? Never mind how you might feel about that but consider how much pleasure it would give Him!

In **Psalms 15:1** and **24:3**, the psalmist poses an important question: Who is righteous enough to approach God? This is clearly rhetorical because he immediately provides his own answer by providing details of good (and bad) character traits which will please (or won't please) the Lord.

LORD, who may abide in Your tabernacle?
Who may dwell in Your holy hill
He who walks uprightly,
And works righteousness,
And speaks the truth in his heart;
He who does not backbite with his tongue,
Nor does evil to his neighbour,
Nor does he take up a reproach against his friend;
In whose eyes a vile person is despised,
But he honours those who fear the Lord;
He who swears to his own hurt and does not change;
He who does not put out his money at usury,
Nor does he take a bribe against the innocent.
He who does these things shall never be moved.

Psalm 15:1-5 (KJV)

Of course, our righteousness is found in Jesus. But, nevertheless, it pleases God when He finds these character traits in us and this book explores how we might go about developing a godly character.

In Romans 5, the apostle Paul identifies that it is by our life experiences that we develop character:

And not only that, but we also glory in tribulations, knowing that tribulation produces perseverance; and perseverance, character; and character, hope.

Romans 5:3-4

From his own experiences as a Christian, Paul certainly knew all about persevering in the face of tribulation. Check out **2 Corinthians 6:4-10** and **2 Corinthians 11:22-33** for a catalogue of Paul's tribulations.

Our characters will be developed, for better or for worse, for good or for bad, by our life experiences whether those experiences be bad (as in Paul's case) or good.

It is, therefore, the intention of this book to provide guidance and to help us in the development of our godly characters regardless of whatever our life experiences may throw at us.

Chapter 1

Personality, Gifting and Character

If you think about it for more than a fleeting moment, it seems like character is becoming less and less important to our world. However, it is very important to God and so we must consider it, learn from it and live our lives by it. That is the reason for opening up this discussion on developing godly character. By recognising and acknowledging the flaws in the alternatives it enables us to chart a course for change.

On the whole, it is easy to confuse character with gifting and personality. You may hear someone, particularly a celebrity or sports person, declaring that a certain person is a wonderful character. Usually what they mean is that they have a charismatic personality that everyone enjoys and they ignore that person's character as if it is unimportant or secondary in their life.

So many of us look up to such people, even though we normally have no idea what they are really like, because we base our judgment on a sparkling performance at the cinema or a spectacular goal on the football field.

So, at the start of this book let's take a deeper look at each of these basic attributes of a person. Then we can better understand the particular matter we are seeking to develop within us.

Personality

So, to begin, what do we understand by personality? Well you could say that it covers many things. It is the intrinsic you. It is what makes you a unique person that defines you and gives you your individuality. Your personality is what you are born with but it is also shaped by your environment and experiences. So, to that end, personality is continually changing yet remains the same.

Personality is a big issue these days. Every one is seeking self-realisation. Personality is everything in that search. We even go further by seeking out our ancestors. You only have to watch the TV programme Who Do You Think You Are to see how far famous people will go to try and discover themselves. Or we go on a retreat or a course to discover the same. Ultimately we are who we are and for most people that is a take it or leave it situation.

However, that must not be so for us who are followers of Christ.

> *I have been crucified with Christ; it is no longer I who live, but Christ who lives in me;...*
>
> **Galatians 2:20**

So, if Christ is living in us then our personality should be submitted to Him. You may feel that this is impossible. However, that is without taking on board that when we come to Christ our life *has* changed.

PERSONALITY, GIFTING AND CHARACTER

Therefore, if anyone is in Christ, he is a new creation; old things have passed away; behold, all things have become new

2 Corinthians 5:17

It does not mean that everything changes immediately. Although there are some well documented examples of those who have been immediately set free from drugs or alcohol or even stronger than that. What it does mean is that, even if there seems to be no change on the outside, something profound has changed on the inside. This gives us great encouragement to press ahead and give our personality (and from that, our character) to Him because he is living in us and, through the Holy Spirit, will assist us in our endeavours.

These days there are a number of personality type indicators. Businesses regularly subject potential job candidates to them in order to discover background as a way of obtaining the best person for the job.

My wife and I, some years ago, took part in a Myers Briggs personality test on several levels to better understand who we are. The great point about that is we were told there is no right or wrong answer. It just demonstrates to us what we are intrinsically like. So we found out that I am an introvert by nature whereas Julie is an extrovert and gets everyone going by her fun remarks. Even so, it is easy to look at the result and declare "yes but when is he going to change?"

No doubt, these days, there are many others that do the same and I have done several of them. They all assume that you stay that way and cannot change. That is, however, without taking into account what submitting to the transforming power of Christ in us can achieve.

Here is the problem. Personality type is twisted by the world to indicate character. Everyone loves outlandish celebrity behaviour and designer clothes, hairstyles etc. Constantly living it up as if that is the normal way to be. We follow our favourite TV series or person and aim to emulate the personality they are creating, mistaking that for true character.

What we don't do is stop and think, "How does that person's character match up to Jesus' character?" Is everything about that thing or person we admire actually at odds with the lifestyle Jesus wants for us? Is what that person stands for compatible with what Jesus stands for?

I am not talking about not having any fun and becoming a boring individual. It is not a sense of "follow Jesus and be just like me". What I am saying is that we have to go beyond the superficial that we see on the outside of a person and look deeper.

This is explained perfectly when, in I Samuel 16, when God asks Samuel to find a new king for Israel and Samuel was considering the various sons of Jesse:

> But the LORD said to Samuel "Do not look at his appearance or at his physical stature, because I have refused him. For the LORD does not see as a man sees; for man looks at the outward appearance, but the LORD looks at the heart"

I Samuel 16:7

This whole passage shows us the difference of how God sees a person and how man does. Saul had been chosen as king and the people loved him because he was tall and handsome. Yet when it came to his coronation he hid himself among the baggage (**1 Samuel 10:22**).

Ultimately, his character let him down. He did not rise up to be the king he should have been and did not trust in the Lord when it mattered but instead took matters in his own hands. So, the Lord rejected him and instead chose a man (David) after His own heart.

God gives each of us an individual personality. This gives us the essence of what makes us tick and how we respond to the world and others. However, He judges us on character and heart.

To a large extent, each of us is born with our personality but we develop our character, for good or bad. You can be the life and soul of the party or you can be studious and thoughtful. That is your personality. But how you react when someone (Mum or spouse or friend) asks you to put out the rubbish or to wash the dishes is down to character development. We forfeit one and promote the other, often the wrong one. We have all seen examples of parents promoting individual expression in their kids when we all know that, underneath, their behaviour leaves a lot to be desired.

Gifting

The idea of gifting encompasses a number of different traits but in order to help us here let me give you a simple definition that assists us in tackling this point.

To be endued with any power or faculty. Something given or bestowed.

Noah Webster's 1828 Dictionary

Now, this equally applies to natural or spiritual gifts or talents.

Great sway is placed upon gifting, especially in charismatic Christian circles, so let me first say something here.

Gifting is good and important. It can be a large part of your unique contribution to the world. It is what you have or are given to achieve your purpose in life. Nevertheless you still have to nurture it in order for it to properly be of use.

It is easy to substitute gifting for character especially as that is what we so often see on the outside and admire or aspire to. Then we get confused if a gifted individual or Christian falls or fails. We are looking on the outward appearance rather than what is going on inside.

There is a well known phrase which states:

Gifting will get you there, but only character will keep you there.

Let me give you some examples:

Johann Strauss 1 was gifted in music and we know that he composed famous waltzes with great success. However, he treated his wife badly, ran off with a mistress and tried to prevent his son from moving into the same sphere of music composition as himself. He had a great gift but a lousy character.

Johann Strauss 2 was a different person with a much better character and the same gifting. He eventually surpassed his father in prominence.

Didier Drogba, who used to play for Chelsea FC, was a gifted footballer but he was always in trouble, often diving in the penalty box. He always looked mean and made some dreadful tackles. He is not the only one like that. I am sure every football team would identify with an opposition member that reflected the same disposition. I question their character.

Freddie Flintoff, an ex-England cricketer who helped England win The Ashes from Australia a number of years ago. Personality and gifting oozes out of him. His great talent and gift got England to the brink of winning.

However, there was also a famous picture of what happened when the Australians failed by 2 runs to win the 3rd test in the series at Edgbaston in 2005. England won by the narrowest of margins. Brett Lee, the Australian who was batting at the time they lost, was in pieces on the field. Yet the first to go over and commiserate with him was Freddie Flintoff. He got down on his knees and genuinely went to console him. That takes character because it takes you out of self. That does not come overnight, it takes time.

I also happen to know, personally, a very well known and gifted preacher from the USA who is often either appreciated or admonished for his fiery bold style of preaching. Yet, outside of that anointing, I know him to be a quiet, thoughtful, kind and generous man, a trait that he carries but many people are unaware of it. We must bear that in mind when we make a character judgment about someone we do not really know.

Character

So, let's finally consider character and the difference it should make for us as believers.

Character is a quality that you develop over your life, good or bad. So, it has to do with your value system and your choices.

DEVELOPING GODLY CHARACTER

Oswald Chambers, in his book, *Biblical Ethics*, describes character as:

The standard of authority within ourselves. A source of power and not a limitation.

Ask yourself what standard you hold to inside yourself. What values and principles do you follow and practice that are different to what shows on the surface. It governs the way you do life.

Some of your character is going to come from learnt principles from parents or shared principles with friends. That is why you need to choose friends wisely, especially if you are young. What you allow to influence you as a young person can have a major effect on how you turn out later in life.

The character or value systems of those you hang around with or admire really matters because part of who they are will rub off on you. Take a long hard look at this and ask yourself: is that person or that thing or that activity a benefit or a hindrance to my long term character and the kind of person I want to be?

It also comes from your own personal choices and values. What you place upon yourself or allow in your life affects you as a moral (or immoral) thinking being. It is the source of your conscience or lack of it.

Some years ago I was working in Bristol, UK, for a big accountancy firm. Regularly, at lunchtime, I, along with many other business people, would walk towards the city centre to buy sandwiches etc. On one occasion I was some way off a very bedraggled and rough looking homeless girl who was sitting on the pavement asking for food. As I got nearer I noticed a very well dressed business woman stop and engage her in conversation. This was not unusual, until I observed the business woman completely step out of her expected behaviour and get right down onto the pavement next to her in order to identify with the plight that this girl was in. I have never forgotten that and it taught me a big lesson. If you have developed the right values and way of thinking then your actions will not be tempered by apparent adverse circumstances because it appears like the wrong thing to do. Rather, you will act according to the values that have grown and flourish on the inside of you. In many ways this is the essence of what we are considering in these pages and serves to demonstrate the possibility of what we can achieve in our own lives.

Now, it doesn't take much for me to point out how that works from a Christian perspective. When you accept Christ, your spirit is changed but your character is not automatically transformed.

Getting born again is the most important event in your life but the daily process of change that comes from submitting and yielding to God has no substitute and we underestimate it.

We must not forget the transforming power of Christ. There are many examples of people who change some things instantly as a result of receiving Jesus on the inside of them. You can probably all identify with that to a larger or smaller extent. Yet, at the same time, we are all aware of issues we have to work on to be truly Christlike and that is a lifelong process.

Our aim should be to work to change our character so that it falls in line with God's choices and values.

"But seek first the kingdom and His righteousness, and all these things will be added to you."

Matthew 6:33

Or as someone I know says "God's way of doing and being right".

I then want to show you something else that demonstrates how important this is and how transformation is a process.

Noah Webster's definition of character includes the following:

A mark made by cutting or engraving as on stone, metal or other hard material. Or a mark or figure made by stamping or impression as on coins.

Noah Webster's 1828 dictionary

So for us there is a sense that what we develop in us becomes the qualities impressed by nature or habit. This distinguishes you from others. Your character is formed by a cutting into you or your soul on the inside and it leaves an impression on the outside wherever it goes. Most often we, as individuals, are the last to see it because it has become such an intrinsic part of us. That means, wherever you go you are never separated from your character, like it or not.

That helps us if we are going to develop godly character. It involves choosing willingly the change process of creating new marks and impressions based on godly ways and leaving old ones that are not.

Chapter 2

Dealing with the Rubbish

We have spoken of our character in terms of qualities in our life, our choices and values. We understand that it is a standard that we hold within ourselves and that our character will always leave a mark or stamp on our life and on other peoples lives.

As I was planning and preparing to write this book, at the back of my mind I was thinking, why am I going down this route right now? What do I need to put over that will help us to see the value of looking at this?

I sensed the Lord say that it was so we can become more robust in our lives. So many times we lead up and down lives, strong in some parts and weak in others. So often we don't face our character flaws. We tend to just say, "Well that's what I'm like, and I cannot change".

The problem is, as a result, most people do not change and we end up not leading such a full life because of it. Also, choosing to ignore an issue can hold us back. It can and will have an effect on those we know or have dealings with on a regular basis. We are often the last to recognise an issue in us even though everyone else can see it plainly.

So, if we are going to take our spiritual character seriously we have to look to build or construct some godly principles that will hold fast through all the ups and downs that life will always throw at us.

Lessons from Nehemiah

Nehemiah is a favourite biblical book of mine. But then I say that about so many books in the Bible. In this one we see Nehemiah returning to the broken down city of Jerusalem and, despite much opposition, he manages to rebuild the city in only 52 days. However, as the preface to this book states in my NKJV Bible, the task of reviving and reforming the people of God within those walls demanded years of Nehemiah's godly life and leadership.

I want to draw a parallel between physically building walls and building and developing character out of the ruins that an ungodly life can leave. In doing so I want to draw your attention to Nehemiah chapter 4. In the previous chapters we find that numerous families and nobles begin the construction of Jerusalem's gates. Together they build them up in sections. Some more carefully than others and some even refused to have anything to do with it.

Perhaps these are typical and maybe understandable reactions that are replicated even as you read this book. You may see the need and make a start or you may toss the book away on the basis that you do not need to change. That is okay but I would encourage you to press on.

In Nehemiah 4 a man called Sanballat heard that the Jews were rebuilding the wall and was indignant saying...

"What are these feeble Jews doing? Will they fortify themselves? Will they offer sacrifices? Will they complete it in a day? Will they revive the stones from the heaps of rubbish—stones that are burned?"

Nehemiah 4:2

His friend Tobiah then attempts to ridicule them and undermine their morale with verbal abuse by claiming that even if a fox should walk on the walls they will fall down. It seems that the task was impossible and the enemy impossible, but I love the little phrase in verse 6 of that same chapter,

So we built the wall,

Nehemiah 4:6

There are some important spiritual principles here if we are to build our wall of godly character.

Expect Opposition and Incredulity

People won't believe you when you say you are working on your character.

The devil does not want you to do that. He would love to make it worse or at the least have you stay where he has got you to right now. The world will not understand the point. If you tell them "Well I'm just improving my golf swing" or "I am developing my fitness levels" then everyone thinks that is great. They envy your determination and perhaps even get inspired to do it themselves.

However, if you say "Well, I'm working on my character" they may laugh and scorn. Underneath though, perhaps they are challenged because, ultimately, pressing through will lead to more godly success in your life. You can approach this just as positively as if you were working on your physical fitness levels. Bear in mind, however, that if you take this decision to build spiritual and soulish strength in your life the devil will not like it and bring opposition in a number of forms. The encouragement I can give is that it is worth persevering because it will make a difference to every area of your life

For bodily exercise profits a little, but godliness is profitable for all things,

1 Timothy 4:8

There is Always Rubbish to Deal With

In Nehemiah, the leaders recognised there was danger from the enemy but also that the wall could not be completed because of the rubbish.

"...there is so much rubbish that we are not able to build the wall."

Nehemiah 4:10

Notice that there was rubbish in and among the good stones. Although they were building, the rubbish was getting in the way and it was leaving them vulnerable to the enemy. They couldn't build as fast as they would like and there were lots of holes in their defences.

Does that sound familiar if we consider it on a on a spiritual level?

In order to overcome this, Nehemiah did two things. He set men with armour to watch and protect the builders and he also worked to deal with the rubbish.

In the context of character, rubbish is waste matter (ungodly ways of thinking or acting based on our our past way of life) that clogs up and holds back the building of our godly character. So, we must deal with it.

Here is an important thought. None of us starts with a clean sheet as far as our character is concerned. It is like a special sheet that looks blank and perfect but there is invisible writing underneath and given the right conditions it will show through.

In the same way, unless we do something about it, our old life will show through, in particular when we are under stress.

However, our spirit does start with a clean sheet so what we do have is a fresh opportunity to work on our soulish realm with fresh eyes and heart.

In the picture that I used in Nehemiah, the purpose behind removing the rubbish was so that it was then easier to see the good stones, keep them, throw out the bad, and that helped them to build the walls stronger and quicker.

With that in mind let's take a look at some ways in which we can deal with our rubbish and then work on the good potential that is there.

By Neglect

This principle is based on the premise that what we feed will grow and what we will neglect won't. If you have a plant in your house, there is a different result if you nourish it, feed it and water it than if you ignore it and leave it to its own devices. If you choose the latter (or rather forget to do the former, as I am sure many of us have done) it will begin to wilt and fade. Eventually it dies off. You removed or destroyed it, not by administering weed killer, just by neglect. The same is true of our spiritual lives. If we concentrate and put our efforts on godly things then these will flourish and thrive and, as the result of neglect, the ungodly, will wither and die.

Colossians provides us with an excellent way we can apply this principle:

Set your mind on things above, not on things on the earth.

Colossians 3:2

We can also apply the following:

Finally, brethren, whatever things are true, whatever things are noble, whatever things are just, whatever things are pure, whatever things are lovely, whatever things are of good report, if there is any virtue and if there is anything praiseworthy—meditate on these things.

Philippians 4:8

So, we have guidelines as to what we are to concentrate on as a result of Jesus being in our life.

Colossians 3:5-7 tell us that we need to put to death certain things and gives a list of things. Additionally, verses 8 and 9 say the same thing in the context of putting off the 'old man'. That gives us a clue as to how to deal with some of our rubbish.

If we put something off we just let it go. Think of your past life like an old garment that when Jesus comes in your life you just let that old thing slip off your shoulders and you put on a new garment. The same can apply to old ways as we just let them go. That is removal by neglect.

Some of our character flaws are not resolved by facing them, or praying about them. Doing so may have a tendency to cause you to brood on it and, before you know it, that thing is amplified more than needs be as you find yourself going over it again and again. No one is immune. We all have things we should not think about and we can be sure the devil will try to be sure we do. Resolutely neglecting that thought and allowing it to decline in its centrality in our life will make a major difference. We do that by concentrating on the opposite i.e. "things above".

Walking in the Spirit

To some extent this could be seen as an extension of the previous section on neglect. But, I believe it is really powerful if we can apply it.

> *I say then: Walk in the Spirit, and you shall not fulfil the lust of the flesh.*
>
> **Galatians 5:16**

This is great practical advice from Paul. He doesn't say "sort out the lust of the flesh then you will walk in the Spirit". Instead he instructs us to let it go by placing our focus on the things of the Spirit.

I remember when I first read this scripture. Revelation hit me like a train! Up until then it had seemed like the whole of my Christian life had been hard going, bouncing from one thing I had to deal with and then another cropped up. Now I realise that the Lord has provided another way with the help of the Holy Spirit that He has placed in us. If we can just let go and focus on the things of God we can walk in a different kind of victory. It lets me know that it is possible to have a "walk in the Spirit" that transcends our previous experience of life before Christ.

Doing this is both spiritual and practical. For example:

> *But the fruit of the Spirit is love, joy, peace, long-suffering, kindness, goodness, faithfulness, gentleness, self control. Against such there is no law.*

Galatians 5:22-23

Fruit implies that there has been growth and change. As we begin to walk in the Spirit we may notice that some fruit springs up instantly, while other fruit takes time. However, if we press through in applying this principle I am convinced there will be a steady change in our Christian walk. As we do, some of our rubbish is removed but we have been focussing on the things of the Spirit, so, we do not notice the change. It is a win-win situation.

By Repentance

I have included this separately as a distinct area with which we have to deal and we cannot do so by applying the principles in the last section. Sin is something that we cannot neglect. We have to deal with it and the way we do is to repent.

Shortly after I gave my life to the Lord I distinctly remember an incident where I had been resolutely witnessing to a person at work. To my surprise she turned round and said "Call yourself a Christian when you are swearing all the time". I was shocked but I realised she had pointed out a character flaw, some rubbish in my life that I was totally unaware of. Not only that, I realised there was sin in my life and it needed dealing with. I remember that night going home and getting before the Lord, repenting and asking Him to help me deal with it. Over the next few months I recall that, somehow, change came in my life as I focused more on the life of God in me and so swearing became a thing of the past. It saddens me now when I hear believers use bad language as if it is normal when in fact it is sin. That is because I know that is something that can be dealt with by repentance.

Repentance is a powerful weapon we have as believers that we often fail to recognise. It was a key part of Jesus' ministry.

> *From that time Jesus began to preach and say "Repent, for the kingdom of heaven is at hand."*

Matthew 4:17

> *"I say to you likewise there will be more joy in heaven over one sinner who repents than over ninety-nine just persons who need no repentance.*

Luke 15:7

We have a somewhat stereotyped view of repentance when in fact it simply means "think again" or "change your thinking". All of us can identify with the need to repent and change at the point we make Jesus our saviour and Lord. However, we have a unique position as believers that when we sincerely repent on anything it *will* be forgiven us and the slate wiped clean. I used this powerfully in my example about swearing but it is something we can all apply more regularly.

I am sure that we will all go through the Christian journey and from time to time, as a result of, for example, reading the bible, or hearing a sermon, discover something that we felt was acceptable and now realise is just plain wrong. If we are going to change our character then we must act in repentance.

In considering this I challenge you today to get before God and let him show you what areas of your character you need to work on and then start practising. It is far easier than having someone point it out to you. Now I am not saying have a witch hunt of yourself and start imagining a problem that is not there. Most of us don't need to go navel gazing. We already have a good idea if we are honest about it. So just run with it and don't get all bogged down. Stay open to Him.

By Making a Sacrifice

In the Sermon on the Mount, Jesus says:

> *"If your right eye causes you to sin, pluck it out and cast it from you; for it is more profitable for you that one of your members perish, than for your whole body to be cast into hell."*

Matthew 5:29

Strong words from Jesus but with an important point. Sometimes we just have to recognise that what we are doing is rubbish, pick it up and throw it away to clean the place up just as the Jews did in Nehemiah's day. In a way you could say that is a sacrifice. In this analogy from Jesus, plucking an eye out was a sacrifice but not doing so was preventing someone getting to their ultimate goal. To that extent sacrifice here is not just a chastening thing but an act of worship. Worship means that I choose to give back to God the best He has given me and in doing this He makes it His and mine forever.

You know the best God has given you is the right to yourself with all your idiosyncrasies. What He wants is to allow our self to be rightly centred in personal passionate devotion to Him.

As we sacrifice to Him we are transformed in our nature and our character in the spiritual. That involves not only praying but also performing and leading a disciplined life.

I beseech you therefore, brethren, by the mercies of God, that you present your bodies a living sacrifice, holy, acceptable to God, which is your reasonable service.

Romans 12:1

To give weight to the discussion above, the Amplified Bible for this verse adds on the end "and spiritual worship."

So often it is not the wrong things that we have to change and give up but the good things that hold us back from that which is better. Will I give up the best I have for the best Jesus has? There may be things we think are okay and we can live with. But God says sacrifice those so you can have the best to enjoy.

In this context, giving something up can be costly, either emotionally or materially, but there is a recognition that in doing so it will change your life for the better. In Acts 19 there is a good example of this where people sacrificed an often lucrative lifestyle for the sake of the gospel.

Also, many of those who had practiced magic brought their books together and burned them in the sight of all. And they counted up the value of them, and it totalled fifty thousand pieces of silver.

Acts 19:19

In the law of the Old Covenant there were many sacrifices. In Jewish understanding this was referred to as 'Qorbanot'. It applied to all sacrifices and offerings, including all those mentioned in the Law. However, they did not see such sacrifice as punitive but rather as an act of worship and something one did in order to get closer to God Himself. This gives credence to the additional words included in the amplified version of **Romans 12:1** (i.e. our "spiritual worship") and is particularly relevant in what we are discussing here as we look to consistently apply principles that will develop a more godly character in us.

By Making Good Choices

The book of Ruth has long been a favourite of mine as it highlights the importance of how choices, good or bad, can influence the destiny of anyone. In chapter 1 we find that there is a famine in the land. A famine of any kind in our life can bring out the best and the worst in us. How we react in the middle of it could most often be as a result of how we see a situation and that can be based on our character and values.

In the story, Elimelech makes a decision purely based on looking after himself and his family. There was food in Moab and so without a second thought he leaves Jerusalem and goes there. Even though Moab is a sworn enemy and, as we find out later in the story, a wealthy relative was around who could have helped him.

Things did not turn out well and he and his sons all died in Moab. His wife, Naomi, made a choice to return to Jerusalem and face the consequences. She gave both of her daughters-in-law an opportunity to stay. Orpah did but Ruth had a different heart and had clearly, by then, learned some things about God, even if it was sketchy. In a famous passage she says...

"Entreat me not to leave you, Or to turn back from following after you; For wherever you go, I will go; And wherever you lodge, I will lodge; Your people shall be my people, And your God, my God. Where you die, I will die, And there I will be buried. the LORD do so to me, and more also, If anything but death parts you and me."

Ruth 1 16-17

Of course, Ruth went back to Jerusalem with Naomi, even though it appeared that everything was against her as a Moabite woman in enemy territory. But God saw her heart, her character, and her new value system. In the end, He ensured she met up with Boaz, the man who was a relative of Elimelech. She married him and had a son, Obed who was in the bloodline of both David and Jesus.

It could be said in both cases that this choice came out of a desire, good or bad. It very much reflects the heart of what you delight in.

Delight yourself also in the LORD, And He shall give you the desires of your heart.

Psalm 37:4

If you abide in Me, and my words abide in you, you will ask what you desire, and it shall be done for you.

John 15:7

What you determine in your mind and settle in your heart and set yourself towards as a goal comes out of that desire and is enacted by a choice. I have heard it described as "making a quality decision". When you set your heart on developing godly character God will fulfill that desire because you are delighting yourself in Him. You are placing your heart, your life, your character in the hands of God and desiring His will for it rather than what you would do naturally.

As we choose good principles we unconsciously neglect/reject bad ones. A good friend of mine, for example, remembers the time when he first became a Christian. He says "I came out of a destructive lifestyle of drinking and partying. I was surprised to find that some Christians were flirting with such a lifestyle. They hadn't experienced what I had experienced and didn't understand that they were playing with fire. But basically, they were making bad choices".

So, the basis of spiritual construction of character is implicit faith and trust in Him. We are declaring that we choose not to go by our own wits or what we can achieve on our own but by what He can achieve in us. By doing so, our qualities and our choices that form our character become conformed to His choices, His character, His way of doing things. What is more, we don't approach that change reluctantly as if we are losing something. We don't take the view "Well I suppose I had better change". If we take that view we never will. No, it has to be part of a design and plan for our lives because our delight is in Jesus. When we have that heart, that attitude, what is built and developed in us is a precious thing that will bring victory in every area of our life.

Therefore we begin to make a new mark. The rubbish in our lives is removed and we begin to replace things with good solid spiritual traits and qualities that will last for all eternity.

Chapter 3

What We Develop in Us

So far we have established the difference between personality and character. We also can see the importance of dealing with the rubbish that has accumulated in our lives throughout our life.

Now let's take a look at starting to develop a godly character within us.

Noah Webster's Dictionary defines develop as:

To unfold, lay open or unravel

Noah Webster's 1828 dictionary

The Concise Oxford Dictionary has a further definition, which is particularly relevant when it comes to growing in godly character:

To bring or come to an active or visible state of maturity.

Concise Oxford Dictionary

Ephesians 4:13 carries a note that reflects this truth. The five fold ministry is given to the body of Christ to equip us...

...till we all come to the unity of the faith and of the knowledge of the Son of God, to a perfect man, to the measure of the stature of the fulness of Christ;

Ephesians 4:13

That seems like an impossible task, knowing ourselves as we do, but we must be capable of attaining to it otherwise it would not be placed in this passage. We can come to maturity. We can grow in character. The heart's desire of the Father is that we are edified or built up.

Luke, chapter 8, contains a pertinent phrase that supports this premise. As Jesus is explaining about the sower sowing the word He says that the seed fallen among thorns are those who...

"...bring no fruit to maturity."

Luke 8:14

Maturity is the decided aim of Christ working in us. Maturity in character will only come by the process of development and a decision not to be distracted by other things. In other words it has to be a focus of our life.

Here is another definition of develop:

Convert to a new purpose so as to use its resources more fully.

Concise Oxford Dictionary

That is a powerful thought. The resources of heaven are available to us as believers. If we desire to grow we can tap into that resource and it will change us. However, we have to be prepared to see the potential and the possibility of what it will do for us and how it will open up new things to us.

A few years ago we were living along a main road in our city. Just across the road from us was an old building that had once been a pub. We were glad when it closed as there were often loud music noises coming from it on a weekend that we could hear and it regularly kept us awake at night. Eventually it was pulled down and the site was cleared. It was earmarked for residential development. When you saw the site with the old building you could not see the potential. Once the site was cleared there was a huge area, not utilised, that you could not see before and it was obvious that there was plenty of space for housing. Those houses were subsequently built and the area transformed. The same potential exists with our life and our heart if we are open to see the possibilities.

Event or Process.

When we come to Christ it is the most important event in our life. However, we forget or don't realise there may have been a process that led to that decision.

It may be someone has been praying constantly for us. There may have been unusual circumstances, or even traumatic events that have culminated in our decision to accept Christ into our life. We do not always recognise this at the point of our conversion. Accordingly, it is easy to think that everything in our life changes immediately. If only it did, we might say. Wisely, with experience, we realise this is not the case and probably that is a good thing. Fruit in our life takes time. It is not an overnight sensation.

That said, I know, as I have said earlier, there are well documented examples of people who have radically changed in an instant, often miraculously at the point of receiving Jesus in their lives. This, indeed would be true of Paul, himself, as a result of the Damascus road experience in Acts 9. What is obvious in Paul's case is that this was an event in a longer term process that God was in control of and planned for Paul's life. Paul responded and so began a series of events, that are well documented in scripture, that changed Paul and changed our lives in due course.

Nevertheless, whether good or bad, it's taken us from the time we were born up until now to get our characters to the point they're at today. So, it's not unreasonable to assume that it may take as much time again to develop godly character in us.

In the illustration I gave about the old building site being cleared, if I told you that within a week of clearance there was a new house or two on the site how keen would you be to go live there? After all, it would be cheap at the price. No, you wouldn't because you would know that it is not possible to build something solid and permanent in that time frame. You would rightly question the workmanship and the quality of the materials used.

In the same way, when you come to Christ would you expect instant change? If you consider it carefully the answer would be no. It takes time even if some things change rapidly because God is working in you. This is especially true when we are applying new principles that we are receiving on a daily basis in order to become more Christlike.

Therefore, godly character development is not an event in itself. It is primarily a development and growth process in your life. The problem is when people want counsel on issues that are character forming they so often want an event based answer. Perhaps they want an instant prayer that solves it or hands laid on so they fall out under the power of the Holy Spirit and get up transformed. Or they expect writing on the wall and angels river dancing on the duvet. We love all that don't we. However, in fact it takes a quality decision to change, which is an event followed by a consistently applied process. This way we gradually and steadily walk out of that issue, which has maybe dogged us for a long time, and which we thought we had to live with. Rather, we begin to develop something new that is long lasting to maturity. Do you understand what I am saying because it will really help you establish some important principles in your life?

If you want to follow this up further I would recommend reading Paul Scanlon's book *Events Versus Process* as it brings this whole area to life.

In **Matthew 7:15-23** Jesus has some strong words that help to bring this into sharper focus. He gives a contrast that we can apply to our character. Jesus dealt with those whose claims were based solely on events like casting out demons, prophecy and working of wonders. He contrasted that to those who were consistently fruit bearing. So, we should not just go for an eventful life but a fruitful life. That is a challenge to many Christians where gifting is highlighted and championed to the exclusion of fruit.

In reality we need to work with a combination punch of event and process.

At a later point in the book I am going to provide some examples of character areas that we can all develop. These fall in three major categories. As you read them you may be powerfully impacted by the Holy Spirit and determine to go forward at an alter call during a service in your local church to deal with that area because you recognise the need and want to change. So you go forward and are prayed for and very moved in the meeting.

Is that event of itself going to change you? It may do but not necessarily. What it will do is give you the impetus to start hearing God and steadily reading the word and acting on what it says so you, day by day, put that new thing into practice until it establishes itself as a permanent part of you, takes root and bears fruit in your life.

In **John 5** we find a man lying paralysed in the porches of the pool of Bethesda. An unusual miracle occurred there from time to time. An angel would stir up the waters and whoever jumped in first got healed. However, this particular man could not do so because of his physical condition, which he had been in for many years. Jesus came along and knew he had been like that for a long time. Jesus commands this man to "Rise, take up your bed and walk". I am always astounded by how Jesus gets us to walk in faith. He asked the man to do something he could not do. The miracle happened as the man began to try.

There is, however, a postscript to that amazing event because Jesus then informs the man that the miracle of healing he had experienced was not the end of it. He says to him:

> *"See you have been made well. Sin no more, lest a worse thing come upon you."*

John 5:14

In his case he needed to consistently stop sinning as an on-going process in his life.

If we are to build strong character we must ensure that each life-changing event we experience is interwoven with the growth process of our life. If we don't we will be constantly up and down and not building strength in ourself.

Going to the gym is regarded as a must do 'pastime' these days. If you think about it though, strength and fitness does not come from just going there and having a look around to experience the atmosphere. It comes from going prepared and then consistently week in, week out, working out and exercising until a change happens.

That same thing needs to apply to the development of our character. We have to be consistent in our approach. The problem is that gradual change as a process in our life is not exciting and spectacular but it is what will steadily put us over in life.

I was recently struck by some words while re-reading *The Holiest of All* by Andrew Murray. The opening of chapter 3 is very pertinent to our discussion.

> *We know that whatever a man sets his heart on exercises a mighty influence on his life, and leaves a stamp on his character. He that follows vanity becomes vain. He that trusts in a god of his own fancy will find his religion an illusion. He that sets his heart upon the living God will find the living God take possession and fill his heart*
>
> **Andrew Murray, *The Holiest of All*,**
> **Chapter 3, opening statement**

As we set our heart to make our character align with His character, we will find the same becomes true for us.

There used to be a programme on UK TV called *How Clean Is Your House?* During the course of the show you see two ladies, Kim and Aggie, do an amazing blitz of an absolute mess of a house and change the look instantly by getting rid of all the grime and clutter. However, it won't stay that way unless the person who lives in the house changes their habits and consistently begins to care properly for their home. Neither will your home!! Neither will your spiritual life or your godly character and fruit. That means you have to consistently care for and work on your character.

The Problem of Creating an Event

When God starts a process in our life, with the intention of producing fruit in us and drawing us closer to Him, we need to resist the temptation to help Him out by creating/introducing events of our own which we think are are in keeping with His process.

Genesis 12 describes a tumultuous, life-changing event which occursi n Abraham's life:

> *Now the Lord had said to Abram:*
> *"Get out of your country,*
> *From your family*
> *And from your father's house,*
> *To a land I will show you.*
> *I will make you a great nation;*
> *I will bless you*
> *And make your name great;*
> *And you shall be a blessing.*
> *I will bless those who bless you,*
> *And I will curse him who curses you;*
> *And in you all the families of the earth shall be blessed."*
> **Genesis 12:1-3**

Here was a remarkable thing. God revealed Himself to Abraham and Abraham believed Him and acted accordingly because he recognised this was God so why should he not go.

The Bible then has this to say in Genesis:

And he believed in the LORD, and he accounted it to him for righteousness.

Genesis 15:6

Let's take a step back in this momentous event in Abraham's life. God said to him "I will make". Now, that is a process phrase. The process that God started in Abraham led to the growth of a nation separated to Him and eventually created the circumstances that brought Jesus onto the planet. Yet, we see that, even with that outstanding promise, Abraham followed it for a while but then he realised the planned process required a son and he did not have one because Sarah was barren. So, in their thinking, Abraham and Sarah created an event to bring about a son that was outside of God's process and Ishmael was produced and the world is still suffering from that.

Now, that should teach us something about learning to trust God in the development of our lives. I am sure that all of us have experiences of taking matters into our own hands. It's the "I don't need God on this" syndrome. Eventually it comes crashing down and we are back to casting all our self on God again. We need to learn something from this if we are to steadily grow.

The obvious conclusion is we should trust God to create the events in our lives that will develop us. They should be instigated by Him, not us.

The Power of Process

"The mood of this age is all wrong. Everybody's looking for proof, but your'e looking for the wrong kind. All your'e looking for is something to titillate your curiosity, satisfy your lust for miracles, but the only proof you're going to get is the Jonah proof given to the Ninevites, which looks like no proof at all. What Jonah was to Nineveh, the Son of Man is to this age."

Luke 11:29 (The Message)

In our rush to change, do we ignore the things in our life that God is constantly showing us in the Word and fail to apply them consistently? Jesus places great store on producing fruit and staying with the program. So, we should be watching out for the small things, which may seem irrelevant to us, but they could be important growth points to God.

Adam was born into process. In **Genesis 1:28** we see that everything with which God blessed Adam required a process to achieve. Adam did not see all the events of creation but God wanted him to fall right in and continue the process that had started. Why? because the power of life was in the process of growth that would spread from generation to generation.

Now think about this, raising great children is a process not an event. Too often great store is placed, primarily, on providing awesome events for our kids when, in reality, it is the consistent love, caring, instruction and shaping is what will make the real difference in their growth, peace, prosperity and future? As a result some kids miss out on a vital element in their development and this can have a lasting effect on their life.

So, let's apply that same principle to growing and developing the godly character that we see daily in the word. Let's understand that determining in our heart to consistently walk out a godly life has great power in it.

That walk may not be spectacular, however, it will be consistently supernatural and, what is more, it will bring about solid change and growth in you that will last forever.

In summary, our Christian walk involves a combination of God breathed events which totally transform our way of seeing life. However, that has to be seen in conjunction with a process that involves making quality decisions which, when consistently applied by ourselves, will have the affect of steadily developing the heart of God in us. As we do that, those around us will see a change and realise that we are not playing at this Christian life. It becomes a joy to us because we experience the deep knowing in our own spirit, that only He can provide.

If this has really spoken to your heart and you have already identified some things which you know you need to change then this may be a good opportunity to pause and take them before the Lord before you go any further.

I am not saying that things are going to change instantly but you are making a declaration before God that you are willing to enter into the process and it will develop something stronger and more robust in you than the place that you are at right now.

Father, in the name of Jesus, I bring before you the things in my life that You have highlighted that need to change in my character. I declare today that I am willing to enter into the process of change that is necessary to develop Your heart and character in me. I ask for the guidance of the Holy Spirit to take me on this journey and bring fresh fruit in my life.

Chapter 4

Character Attributes—Spiritual

We have spent some time looking at the 'how to' of developing godly character in us and the importance of seeing this as an ongoing process in our lives spurred on by significant events.

I now want to take a look at some character attributes that the Bible talks about because we should be aiming and seeking to build them into our life.

Before we do so it's important to understand something. I am not saying that Jesus expects us to have all these immediately on board in our life. They are all things to aim for and they may take time. Some you will look at and have a strong handle on, some you may be struggling with, some you may not even have thought about.

One thing is for sure, I am not expecting a kind of superman status right now. I remember a number of years ago we were at the Eiffel tower and I was messing around trying to impress Julie by taking a superman pose and pretending. All I got for my efforts was catching my new leather jacket on the railings and finding a button fly off down about 300 feet. So don't try and be a poser on this, it rarely works. Be real.

Yes, furthermore, I count everything as loss compared to the possession of the priceless privilege (the overwhelming preciousness, the surpassing worth, and supreme advantage) of knowing Christ Jesus my Lord and of progressively becoming more deeply and intimately acquainted with Him [of perceiving and recognising and understanding Him more fully and clearly]. For His sake I have lost everything and consider it all to be mere rubbish (refuse, dregs), in order that I may win (gain) Christ (the Anointed One),

Philippians 3:8 (AMPCE)

Get a hold of the idea in this scripture and determine to be progressive. Be open to change.

I am going to split these attributes into 3 sections, Spiritual, Emotional and Tangible. That gives us an acronym of SET which should make it easy to remember. These attributes are not exhaustive. My intention is that, in each section, they will give you a flavour of godly character attributes. More could be said about each one and other definitions could be added. The ones I have chosen will, hopefully, provide a framework for you to get hold of the basics.

Spiritual Character Attributes

a) Holiness

I suggest, at the outset, that holiness is the most important character attribute that we should be aspiring to. All the others in these next three chapters flow from holiness. Therefore, let us consider it in some detail here.

I once did a study on holiness as I was moved by God's commandment to us in these verses:

For I am the LORD who brings you up out of the land of Egypt, to be your God. You shall therefore be holy, for I am holy.

Leviticus 11:45

because it is written, "Be holy for I am holy"

I Peter 1:16

I discovered there are around forty different words used in scripture for holiness. However there are two basic words, one Hebrew word from the Old Testament, and one Greek word from the New Testament.

The Hebrew word is *qadash* from the root of *qodesh.* It means:

To set aside, consecrate, or to make holy. Implying moral and ethical excellence

Holman Treasury of Key Biblical Words.

The Greek word is *hagiasmos.* In essence it means:

Separation from everything ceremonially impure

Holman Treasury of Key Biblical Words.

These definitions are relevant for us, but as I investigated all the many aspects of holiness I was struck by a comment in *Eardmans Bible Dictionary* describing holiness as the root or core of God's being. In other words, it is the very essence of God Himself. This definition satisfied my curiosity. All the various attributes of God; love, mercy, grace, covenant and all His various names can be encapsulated in that one word. It is not surprising, then, that God is asking us to be holy. In effect He is saying to us we should be like Him. It means that we should be consecrated or set apart and have our heart conformed to the image of God and our life regulated by divine precepts.

> "For you are a holy people to the LORD your God; the LORD your God has chosen you to be a people for Himself, a special treasure above all the peoples on the face of the earth."
>
> **Deuteronomy 7:6**

Although this primarily related to the Jewish nation, we also are a holy people as we are grafted in to the vine as believers (**Romans 11:17**).

In Paul's letter to the Colossians we read this:

> Therefore, as the elect of God, holy and beloved, put on tender mercies, kindness, humility, meekness, longsuffering;
>
> **Colossians 3:12**

That implies there is a consequential action of of being holy.

We have to develop in us a daily separation from the ways of the world. We have to be daily consecrating ourselves to God. Now, that doesn't mean we walk around with our nose in the air looking holier than anyone else like the old idea of what a monk or nun looked like. We should note at this point that Jesus, Himself, was in the world but not of the world.

No, it is a decision that we make consistently of the kind of life we will lead. There will always be a temptation to be worldly, to act like we are not a holy people. We are not immune.

That implies there is a consequential action. We don't go around with a halo or a force field so everything un-holy stays away or bounces off us. We have to make a choice to be holy towards God in our spiritual life. Calling oneself a Christian and having that one off experience of coming to Christ is not going to cut it as I clearly demonstrated earlier over my swearing incident. We have been made sons and daughters of God and we walk in freedom but we have to choose daily to be a disciple and follow after Him. This is not meant to be a legalistic directive but a determination that as we aim to follow this path we are coming ever closer to the heart of God.

b) Godly

But know that the Lord has set apart for Himself him who is godly;

Psalm 4:3

teaching us that, denying ungodliness and worldly lusts, we should live soberly, righteously, and godly in the present age,

Titus 2:12

Again, in these passages we can see how God treats us as being godly, but then reminds us how we should live. That is good news. We can enjoy the knowledge that we are special to God. Yes, we should rejoice but at the same time there is a consistent character that has to come through.

DEVELOPING GODLY CHARACTER

Noah Webster defines godly as:

Living in obedience to God's commands, from a principle of love to him and reverence for his character and precepts;
Noah Webster's 1828 Dictionary

Oh-oh, that means I have to live godly 24/7, even when I'm not in church and even when I'm on my own and no one is looking. No, I do that just because I love God and I am so thankful for what he has done for me and the very fact that He has chosen me. It is a tall order but one we must aim for if we are to really develop and grow in godliness.

Harper's Bible Dictionary provides us with some further helpful words that describes "godly" as:

...the English translation of a Greek root (also translated as 'religion, religious,' 'piety, pious,' 'devotion, devout,' or 'worship, worshipper') common in the NT world to describe respect for Greek and Roman gods and for the orders of society. This may be why the term seldom appears either in the Septuagint (LXX) or in the NT. Biblical writers prefer such words as 'righteousness,' 'faith,' 'steadfastness,' 'holiness,' etc., to describe the faith and life pleasing to God. In the OT, true godliness or piety usually finds expression as covenant loyalty, steadfastness, faithfulness, kindness, goodness, or holiness:
Harper's Bible Dictionary

Clearly, godly is close in likeness to holiness. The various words in this quote reflect the heart of why we are looking at developing godly character. It leads us on to another attribute, mentioned by Harper.

c) Devout

Noah Webster provides a good definition of devout:

Yielding a solemn and reverential attention to God in religious exercises, particularly in prayer.

Noah Webster's 1828 Dictionary:

Acts 8:2 talks of devout men carrying Steven to his burial. The NKJV's use of the word "devout" in this verse is in keeping with most of the major translations. However, we gain a fuller understanding of the meaning by considering the alternatives of "godly" or "pious" or "reverent" which are used by some other translations.

And they devoted themselves to the apostles' teaching and the fellowship, to the breaking of bread and the prayers.

Acts 2:42 (ESV)

This verse describes the commitment of the earliest believers and therefore gives a glimpse into the behaviour of devout believers.

Now, you may not have thought of yourself as a very devout person. Perhaps you thought that was outdated thinking or reserved for monks and priests who had nothing better to do all day. But what we see here is that it should be a character trait of our spirit.

It does not mean that you lead a boring life, always in books and never going out on the town or enjoying life. What it does mean is that in the midst of living life you pay correct attention to God and His ways.

It might not be the coolest thing to be known as devout but at the end of the day ask yourself this: Who am I pleasing, God or the world?

d) Knowing His Voice

"But He who enters by the door is the shepherd of the sheep. To him the doorkeeper opens, and the sheep hear His voice; and He calls His own sheep out by name and leads them out. And when He brings out His own sheep, He goes before them; and the sheep follow Him, for they know His voice. Yet they will by no means follow a stranger, but will flee from him, for they do not know the voice of strangers."

[27] "My sheep hear My voice, and I know them, and they follow Me.

John 10:2-5; 27

Let's study this passage a moment. It is saying we should follow Him, Jesus, because we know His voice and we hear it.

This is not a one-off event. It is not meant to refer only to when you heard and responded to His call and you got born again. It is clear from this passage that Jesus is constantly wanting to show us the right path and the safe place to be. In response, therefore, we have to be attuned to His voice and stay listening on a constant basis.

"Your ears shall hear a word behind you, saying, this is the way, walk in it."

Isaiah 30:21

This is a profound thought, but how do we respond? To follow means to accompany, go along with, go the same way with, follow one who precedes. In other words we want to be constantly on the same roadway with Jesus. Ultimately, we follow Him because we are His sheep. We know Him because we recognise His voice. By following Him and His voice we know where to go.

That is not an easy task. Have you tried it recently? It is easy to veer off when some other distraction comes along. For that reason, Jesus wants us to be attentive to Him and to follow Him. Not because he is a spoilsport or a killjoy but because He is looking out for our best interests. We have to decide that He knows what is best for us and follow after him. This is real character development because it requires us to hear and choose even if we cannot see the outcome. It is simple trust, nothing more and nothing less. That is faith in action and the Bible tells us that is how we should live.

e) Led by the Spirit

In the chapter on dealing with the rubbish, we brought up the following verse as a key to the process of change. Here we repeat it as an obvious attribute of the spiritual life.

For as many as are led by the Spirit of God, these are the sons of God.

Romans 8:14

As believers we all probably rest in the fact that we are seen as sons and daughters of God. However, when we look at this carefully we learn that the word "led" here is a present continuous in the Greek. It has the sense of continually being led.

The sense here is not just to the obvious objective commands. "Do this, don't do that". Instead it is being sensitive to the promptings of the Holy Spirit throughout the day. Such promptings will never encourage us to act contrary to scripture. If we refer back to **Romans 8:13**, we see Paul is encouraging us to stop the acts of the flesh. You do this by being progressively led by the promptings of the Spirit and therefore it will make you more completely obedient to God and conformed to His holy standards.

> *I say then: Walk in the Spirit, and you shall not fulfil the lust of the flesh.*

Galatians 5:16

That is a critical verse because it asks us first to walk in the Spirit and when we do we will not fulfil the lusts of the flesh. It is not the other way round. It does not say to deal with the lusts of the flesh then you will walk in the Spirit. That is good news for us but it requires a discipline to do it.

We must recognise that the Holy Spirit is here for us and the more we trust Him then the more we will progress in our spiritual walk with God and the more our character will be formed in us.

f) Fearing God

The book of Acts takes the idea of devout, mentioned earlier, to another level when it talks about Cornelius in **Acts 10:2:**

a devout man and one who feared God with all his household, who gave alms generously to the people, and prayed to God always.

The fear of the Lord is the beginning of wisdom;

Psalm 111:10

In both these scriptures we are not talking about a classic definition of fear as:

an unpleasant emotion caused by exposure to danger

Concise Oxford Dictionary

Quite the contrary, in this context it means:

to fear, revere, be afraid 1a) (Qal): 1a1) to fear, be afraid; 1a2) to stand in awe of, be awed; 1a3) to fear, reverence, honour, respect; 1b) (Niphal): 1b1) to be fearful, be dreadful, be feared; 1b2) to cause astonishment and awe, be held in awe; 1b3) to inspire reverence or godly fear or awe;

Strongs 3372, Brown-Driver-Briggs' Definition

That is the sense in which we apply it to God. In fact, according to the scripture it is all we should fear. We are not to fear anything else.

You know, it also means we don't get involved in jokes about God because He is our Lord and Saviour and we worship and hold Him up in high esteem whenever we get the chance. On that basis we do not shy back from talking about Him because He is everything to us.

g) Hunger for Righteousness

"... Blessed are those who hunger and thirst for righteousness, For they shall be filled. ..."

Matthew 5:6

Let me ask you this: when are you made righteous (or placed into right standing with God)? According to **2 Corinthians 5:21**, it is when we are made righteous in Christ at the new birth. So that means we are righteous now. We do not have to wait until the future when we finally make it to heaven.

So, why does this verse, from the mouth of Jesus Himself, tell us we are blessed if we hunger and thirst after righteousness? It has to be because He wants it to be a consistent attribute of our spiritual character that we are exercising and living in the fullness of on a daily basis. So, craving His righteousness is like the experience we are familiar with when we hunger. It is a strong desire. We just have to eat to satisfy it. Only walking in righteousness will satisfy that spiritual hunger. Then, eventually, we get hungry for the same thing again and desire to stay walking that way. We just have to be like that.

When we are like that it is a consuming passion in our life. It is more than knowing we are righteous, it is walking that life out with Him. Jesus says if you do that you will be full, Hallelujah. You will be full of Him.

So, as we close this chapter, let us be mindful of these spiritual attributes and be determined to sow them and grow them into our life and our character. These are the most important elements of our spiritual growth.

Chapter 5

Character Attributes—Emotional

So, following our acronym of SET, let's turn to some emotional attributes of a godly character. You know, for too long we have been conned into suppressing emotions on the basis that spiritual is everything, and especially "the gifts".

Sometimes we forget that God created us as a whole being: spirit, soul and body. **3 John 2** even speaks about our soul prospering or, to put it another way, being rich in every area of our life (not just financially) and this will effect everything else. Our soul consists of our mind, will and emotions. So, developing emotions in a godly way becomes a vital part of what we should be aiming for as Christians. Conformed to the life and character of God, our emotions will be healthy.

Emotional attributes

a) Loving and merciful

Now, we need to understand that this topic is not talking about what we know as spiritual love, which is a fruit of the Spirit. Remember, we are talking about character so this is relating much more to an active demonstration based upon a lifestyle decision that we are going to live our lives by.

So, that means, no matter what somebody says to you or about you or about a relative or friend or if someone is just plain ugly, being loving and merciful is the way you act. Is that easy? No it isn't. That is why it's all about character.

> *But concerning brotherly love you have no need that I should write to you, for you yourselves are taught by God to love one another;*

1 Thessalonians 4:9

Is that our experience? Do we not need to remind ourselves to love and have mercy because we are doing it automatically without thinking. Or do we have to work at it daily?

> *"...But I say to you, love your enemies, bless those who curse you, do good to those who hate you, and pray for those who spitefully use you and persecute you,..."*

Matthew 5:44

Now, that is taking matters a step further. We are all happy to strive to love better those we already love or are friends with. But loving those who do not treat us well is taking us the extra mile. How many of us do that? What a challenge for building character in us.

Take a look with me at the passage in **Luke 10:25-37.**

The man in question has no problem with loving God. It is always easy to spiritualise it. His problem comes in relation to how he should be to the neighbour. He asks Jesus "who is my neighbour" because he wants to justify his own position which was probably not very charitable to others.

So, Jesus uses an example. He talks about a "certain man". There is no suggestion that this was a parable even though most people would say it was. Jesus may have known about the story personally. So, He gets right to it by describing a mugging, by any other name. We are familiar with the story of the Levite, the priest and the Samaritan and how a sworn enemy of Israel is the one who helps the man and treats him well. Showing that kind of love is a very practical demonstration of what we are talking about here.

In the end, the man can hardly bear to admit who had shown mercy to the one who had been mugged. He certainly couldn't say his name. Now, do we act with the Samaritan kind of love and mercy or is the practical demonstration of what that means, according to Jesus, too much for us also?

*Blessed are the **merciful**, for they shall obtain **mercy**.*
Matthew 5:7 (emphasis added)

When you are merciful, tender and compassionate towards people, you will find the mercy of God is poured upon you. What a way to live. Can we strive for that consistently? Our harsh judgment of people who may mess up is, in effect, judging them, or anyone else for that matter, based upon how we see it. Instead, being merciful helps us to cease from having a critical mindset and causes us to develop a loving heart.

b) Lowly and Meek

These words are an anathema to most modern-day ears. Perhaps it is because for the most part they are not common in every day usage, and therefore misunderstood. Today it might seem as if everyone is out for themselves. The world pushes us and praises those who strive to be first at all costs. It does not care who someone steps over on the way to the top. On the other hand this character trait seems as though we are advocating being a nothing or nobody. Never standing up for yourself. Being ever so humble and a worm in the ground. That is because we have largely lost the spiritual biblical context of these words. So we need to understand them more as they are godly attributes we are encouraged to possess and display.

For example: lowly, in reality, just means "freedom from pride".

Also, as a Greek verb, it means:

being carried off along with; hence *yielding* or *submitting to,*

Oh, that puts a whole new slant on it. That understanding helps us to focus ourselves because it is clearly something we would want to attain to in yielding to God even in the natural way of things.

"Take My yoke upon you and learn from Me, for I am gentle (or meek) and lowly in heart, and you will find rest for your souls."

Matthew 11:29 (parenthesis added)

From that scripture, we can see that "meek" contains the sense of being gentle. It also means you are not easily provoked or irritated (that is an important character trait for us in today's world).

Another definition can be found in Strong's Bible Dictionary:

> *Biblical meekness is not weakness but rather refers to exercising God's strength under His control – i.e. demonstrating power without undue harshness.*
>
> **Strong's 4239**

Everyone, it seems, is angry about everything, ranging from the weather to the person who just cut you up in the car. Oh-oh, I just found I have something to work on. Question: are you easily provoked and do you get irritated? Are you able to demonstrate His power without harshness? Well, remember this is a process of change so that every time you have an opportunity to be like that you begin to do, say and act differently. Then, with the help of the Holy Spirit, you choose that different way, even if it is with clenched teeth at first, until it becomes a part of you. People will notice the change because you are in control and demonstrating a key fruit of the Spirit.

c) Contrite

Contrite is actually defined as someone who has a deep sorrow for sin. It is relevant here because our sin is now in our soulish realm and it reflects an attitude of heart.

> *For thus says the High and Lofty One Who inhabits eternity, whose name is Holy: "I dwell in the high and holy place, With him who has a **contrite** and humble spirit, To revive the spirit of the humble, And to revive the heart of the **contrite** ones..."*
>
> **Isaiah 57:15 (emphasis added)**

We must have that same attitude to sin. It has to be part of our character. Yes we will all miss it, we will make a mistake, we will do wrong, BUT how we respond when we do is a point of character building. If we are quick to repent and seek His forgiveness it keeps a short account with Him because we are declaring it is the way we truly desire to walk and He responds accordingly.

d) Sincere and Pure in Heart

The Greek word *hagnos* is translated as 'pure' and comes from the same root as holy.

> *Beloved, now we are children of God; and it has not yet been revealed what we shall be, but we know that when He is revealed, we shall be like Him, for we shall see Him as He is. And everyone who has this hope in Him purifies himself, just as He is pure.*
>
> **1 John 3:2-3**

Another Greek word *eilikreness* is translated as 'sincere'.

> *that you may approve the things that are excellent, that you may be sincere and without offense till the day of Christ,*
>
> **Philippians 1:10**

The strange thing is, we always seem to know when someone is being insincere. It is somehow built into us. Sincere means honestly with purity of heart and not disguise. How often today do we disguise the truth from people and then have to handle the consequences when the truth gets out? Well, if we determine to walk constantly in the truth and the light then we will not put ourselves in a position that we may regret.

It also means that we are not pretentious. In other words, not putting on airs and graces and not pretending to be somebody that we are not. In reality, if we walk with a pure heart, God will be released to work for us because that is the kind of person He is looking for. The supreme example of that is Jesus. When He was in the middle of the most extreme temptation. He kept pure in Himself even when the devil was out to get Him to do otherwise. That is integrity of heart that we must all grow in more.

e) Blameless, Harmless and Guileless

> *Jesus saw Nathaniel coming to Him, and saith of him, Behold an Israelite indeed, in whom is no guile!*
>
> **John 1:47 (KJV)**

The NIV translates guile as "without deceit". The New Living Translation goes further and translates it as "with complete integrity".

Hopefully, that gives a more accurate, modern meaning to a word that has fallen out of everyday use.

> *that you may become blameless and harmless, children of God without fault in the midst of a crooked and perverse generation, among whom you shine as lights in the world,*
>
> **Philippians 2:15**

Basically, in this section we are not trying to create the idea that someone should become an "harmless as a butterfly" type of character. These words refer to being without fault, walking in integrity and being innocent. Now, these days, that idea is frowned upon. There is an encouragement for everyone to be into something dodgy, as if that is the normal way of doing things. The very thought of growing up with an innocence is hardly talked of. In fact the devil is trying very hard to get rid of innocence in the world. You only have to watch TV for a short period of time and you can see what I mean.

Yet, even then we need to step in a bit deeper. As we are talking about character, being without fault and being innocent does not only refer to a specific incident (e.g. being accused of doing something you did not do) but it is also a lifestyle issue that you consistently apply in your life. To live with integrity is to be always walking in truth, not lying or being out to deceive people (that is where being guileless comes in). It also will be built upon with the kind of conversation you keep with people, the sort of things you allow yourself to watch or indulge in, especially on the media. For example, there are times when someone is "economical with the truth". This is a way of deceit by not telling the full story.

We need to see this is not being a spoilsport or pushing for something that is impossible to do. God wants these things to be a part of you because he wants you safe and protected, full of life and healthy.

You know, it's important to remind ourselves of the very fact that God raised us up for this time because He has confidence that we have the ability to overcome in the midst of everything the devil and the world could throw at us. Consider that for a moment. If you think it's impossible to remain innocent in this generation just remember God caused you to be born in this generation because He knew, ultimately, you have what it takes to be a believer in this time. If you did not, He would have had you born some other time.

So, you have what it takes to walk in this kind of integrity. Yes, it might mean people have a bit of a laugh because you restrict the kind of films you watch and are careful about those with whom you hang around BUT it is all worth it in the end because God is working His glory out in you.

> *being confident of this very thing, that He who has begun a good work in you will complete it until the day of Jesus Christ;*

> **Philippians 1:6**

So, the traits we have just looked at are the areas we must work on because they are ones we have to win. Praise God, we have help in the form of the Holy Spirit and He is constantly on our side and with Him we have the victory now.

Chapter 6

Character Attributes—Tangible

Our final attributes, using our acronym of SET, are what I have, for convenience, termed as tangible ones. *The Oxford Thesaurus* provides us with some alternative words for tangible as: material, real, physical, solid, concrete, substantial and objective, among others. So, they reflect areas that are very solidly pertinent to our everyday life.

First, let me remind us, when we started this study we spoke of character as the standard of authority we have in ourselves and that it is a source of power and not limitation.

So, as we start to look at some very tangible things that can be tough to apply, let's remember that and know that His power is what we are aiming for.

a) Bold and Zealous of Good Works

...the righteous are as bold as a lion.

Proverbs 28:1

who gave himself for us, that He might redeem us from every lawless deed and purify for Himself His own special people, zealous for good works.

Titus 2:14

From these verses we glean understanding that God wants us to be zealous and completely sold out for Him. That can seem like a tall order when there is so much opposition to the gospel and the things of God. Nevertheless, as Proverbs states, we are as bold as a lion. You may not feel like that on a daily basis so it is important, then, to get a hold of it and build this into your character.

Jesus is our supreme example of boldness and zealousness. In fact, this is what the word says in **John 2:13-19**. Notice the boldness in which He answers the Jews. In effect he says "kill me and I come back to life in 3 days". Almost as if He is daring them to do it and He is ready for it. Here, 'bold' means: daring, courageous, intrepid, confident, standing out to view, without fear. Zealous means: passionate ardour in the pursuit of something. Then, an old dictionary I read said "excessive zeal can give rise to enthusiasm!"

We need to remind ourselves that this is godly character. Therefore, we should question any thought that suggests we should not be like this. However, I feel it is important that we differentiate between character and brashness or bravado. How many times have we seen a bold sort of brashness, especially from a preacher. Something spoken may sound good and comes over strong, but somehow there is a falseness to it that is easy to see through and, in truth, is just bravado.

So, we have to be mindful of the traps because this trait is something that is clearly obvious on the outside even though it is a measure of what has been developed on the inside.

Nevertheless, both these things are qualities that the Lord wants us to develop. So, why is that and how do we go about it?

Well, if we are going to have an impact on a world that is in trouble we are going to have to step out of our natural tendency to hold back. We need to see also that not being bold comes ultimately from a heart of fear on the inside and also an unwillingness or lack of confidence to share who we are in Christ and what He has done for us.

What I see is that this character trait, properly developed through practice with the help of the Holy Spirit, will transcend personality. You can be a quiet person, but still bold. You don't have to be someone who goes over the top all the time but you can make a decision to do this and then apply it, gently but firmly, in your daily walk. In doing so, eventually it becomes a part of you and people will notice because there will be a confidence and a security in you. So, steadily, you build it into your character.

b) Faithful, Just and Steadfast

"He who is faithful in what is least is faithful also in much:
Luke 16:10

This is the genealogy of Noah. Noah was a just man, perfect in his generations. Noah walked with God.
Genesis 6:9

And they continued steadfastly in the apostles' doctrine and fellowship.

Acts 2:42

All these scripture quotes contain these words and help to place them in context. These traits are fairly familiar to us in the Christian world and can be found in many other texts. So, you would think that it is something we live and stand by. But, increasingly, you hear of Christians who seem to have a problem with some of these things. So much so that we no longer bat an eyelid when we hear of someone falling or failing. What a contrast to someone like Billy Graham who, at the time of writing this, has just moved to heaven and even the world is crying out "well done good and faithful servant".

Perhaps the reason is because these particular traits require a consistency, Maybe we should stop and think, are we increasingly seeing that many Christians do not see this as so important? If that is the case, let's take a look at them again.

Faithful: firm in adherence to the truth, in service, constant
Noah Webster's 1828 Dictionary

The Greek word *pistos* is defined by Strong's Concordance as meaning:

loyalty to faith; literally, fulness of faith and typically, of believing the faith God imparts.
Strong's Concordance, 4103

Therefore, there is a sense of sticking with something and not giving up, being reliable. Can Jesus rely on you, can the Church rely on you, and can your family rely on you?

Just: true, upright, honest, principled, impartial.
Noah Webster's 1828 Dictionary

So, think of my surprise when a few years ago Julie and I read of a minister who bought a villa and an expensive car for himself on the church credit card. We just have to be more principled in our lives. Not only is this not right but it puts the financial integrity of that ministry into a sharp spotlight. If this has not been your highest priority, especially in financial dealings, then why not covenant with yourself, in other words make a firm commitment for the future, to make it so.

Steadfast: to be constant, firm, steady of mind, unwavering.
Concise Oxford Dictionary

Does anyone identify with a problem in this area? It takes a lot to become steady in our mind and not vacillate and waver all the time. If we make this a priority we will notice a major change in our lives.

These character traits are so important for the kingdom. In many ways they set us apart from the world and I believe we need to stop the rot and be determined to build them into our lives.

c) Obedient, Upright and Watchful

Strong's Concordance defines 'obedience' (Greek, *hupakoé*, 5218) in terms of "submission to what is heard" and "the response to someone speaking".

In itself submission has had a bit of a rough ride, with the idea that someone is forced to submit or be obedient. But It was never intended that way. Submission and obedience is a choice made by the person doing the submission or being obedient. Anything else is wrong. In this context we are talking about being obedient to Christ and His ways. That is a character choice we make. Jesus would never force us. Additionally, it suggests an inbuilt respect for authority. That in itself is a challenge these days. No one seems to respect authority and therefore it can be difficult to get someone to say "yes" when things need to get done. Yet it is a character trait and quality that God seeks highly.

The following passages help to provide clarification by drawing attention to the opposite trait, divisiveness, which can pollute us and draw us away.

> *Now I urge you, brethren, note those who cause divisions and offenses, contrary to the doctrine you learned, and avoid them. For those who are such do not serve our Lord Jesus Christ, but their own belly, and by smooth words and flattering speech deceive the hearts of the simple. For your obedience has become known to all. Therefore I am glad on your behalf; but I want you to be wise in what is good, and simple concerning evil.*

Romans 16:17-19

> *casting down arguments and every high thing that exalts itself against the knowledge of God, bringing every thought into captivity to the obedience of Christ,*

2 Corinthians 10:5

Wow, we know these passage well but what a challenge to actually do it. It's so easy to let thoughts wander and daydream.

Yet, we see here the importance of bringing them into obedience for our own wellbeing. God does not say such things for His own good but for ours because He knows how vital this is for us.

Now, we need also to be able to translate that into our everyday life, both in the Church and in our family and work life. This is all part of being of one heart and mind with Him. This does not mean we become robots but we learn to flow with the heart, vision, DNA and spirit of where we are moving as a Christian community worldwide.

We then link that action to being upright, it acts as a balance. You don't be obedient to something that is clearly going to compromise your integrity but you stay upright and true to the abundant life God has prepared for us. For example In **1 Kings 3:6** We see how Solomon saw uprightness in David who is a great example for us all.

Uprightness means a moral soundness or purity especially in mutual dealings. Why say that? Well you can appear upright and moral in speech but be an absolute terrible person to deal with in business and prepared to do any sort of deal to get your way.

One of the Greek words that upright is derived from translates as 'straight'. In some ways it reminds me of the plumb line that I always use when hanging wallpaper at home. If you don't hang the first piece and make sure it is straight using the plumb line, which hangs from the wall with a weight and is therefore completely vertical, then every other piece will increasingly be on a slant.

It also paints a good picture in relation to how Job is described at the beginning of that book, reflecting the man's heart throughout.

There was a man in the land of Uz, whose name was Job; and that man was blameless and upright, and one who feared God and shunned evil.

Job 1:1

So, it implies there has to be a consistency and integrity in how we conduct ourselves. You need to ask yourself: "How upright am I?" It's a legitimate question and we need to let the Holy Spirit minister to us and allow ourselves to be shaped on this one by His leading.

Finally, in this section, be watchful.

In **Luke 12:35-40** we see Jesus explain to His disciples the importance of staying watchful in a similar manner to when the master comes for a wedding.

Watchful, here, means to be vigilant and attentive. It is applied by Jesus as a parallel to being ready for Christ's return and how, therefore, we should act and behave in anticipation of that. It can equally apply to many other situations. For example, we should be watchful over our children, over our relationships, our language. Also, we should be watchful over our hearts and our mouths as David cries out in the Psalms:

*Set a **guard**, O Lord, over my mouth; Keep watch over the door of my lips.*

Psalm 141:3 (emphasis added)

Jesus expands on this as part of a discourse that Matthew refers to and we know as the sermon on the mount. However, in the similar passage in Luke Jesus says:

"A good man out of the good treasure of his heart brings forth good; and an evil man out of the evil treasure of his heart brings forth evil. For out of the abundance of the heart the mouth speaks.

Luke 6:45

In essence this means we should watch what words, thoughts and lifestyle, we allow to become a part of our belief system. That is because, whether we want to or not, what has accumulated into our heart and thinking, will come out in the things we say because we can't help it.

I guess, over all, much of this boils down to watching that you do live a real, true Christian life in the midst of all the pressures that life will try and throw at you.

d) Undefiled

Blessed are the undefiled in the way, Who walk in the law of the Lord!

Psalm 119:1

Now, I know this sounds like something out of a horror movie and has overtones of physical disease like saying "unclean, unclean" in reverse. However, see this in more depth when looking at the next few verses. You are blessed by keeping His testimonies and seeking Him with a whole heart, having no iniquity and walking in His ways.

Pure and undefiled religion before God and the father is this; to visit orphans and widows in their trouble, and to keep oneself unspotted from the world.

James 1:27

The idea of being unspotted from the world carries the thought of staying clean and whole, walking in purity and integrity. In effect, that flows from guarding your heart. It is an attribute where we determine to keep ourselves free from everything the world would throw at us. Now, that is easy to say but it is not easy to do as distractions and the work of the enemy would constantly try to deflect us from following that purpose.

So, how do we make a stand and do these things?

e) Taught of God

All your children shall be taught of the LORD, and great shall be the peace of your children

Isaiah 54:13

Now, this is a very pertinent passage because it demonstrates the importance of starting down the road early in following after the word of God. In essence, there is no substitute for it.

We must aim to grow and develop our ability to be taught by God constantly and consistently.

We choose to seek after Him and make the choice to change our way to following after His way. We recognise where we stand as we read the word, meditate on it and allow it to penetrate our spirit. We then see what has to change and can take steps to do so. We may never feel we have arrived as there is always more to grow into. As we SET ourselves this as a target we can know that the Holy Spirit will be there to help us, encourage us, guide us and lead us. Then, like the word says, great will be the peace of our children and great will be our peace.

Chapter 7

So, where do we go from here?

The previous chapters have provided us with a series of ways to eliminate poor character and then given us a plethora of points on what forms godly character. None of them are exhaustive and, no doubt, they will have triggered off other points that you could identify. For each point it would be possible to delve down into even more detail. However, I feel that highlighting them, as I have, will have served enough for you to go deeper, if you need to, or research further.

The key, now, is to consider some practical help that will enable you to start and sustain developing those areas of godly character that you identify as needful in your own life. The devil would convince you to look at this whole area pragmatically. Perhaps he will press you into feeling it is so impossible that either you should not bother starting, or make you feel like you would never succeed anyway. If he can do that you may then say "just forget it, I'll stay as I am now because I can't change anything."

So, this is where the serious among us step up to the plate and begin. This is where we have to make a quality decision and, despite how we may feel, make a start. When we just look at ourselves we fail miserably because we are looking in the natural.

God does not see us that way. He is looking at the heart. He sees us from a finished perspective. From **Hebrews 12:2** we learn that Jesus is the author and finisher of our faith.

He will see us through if we begin and look to Him. God is with us. He is not indifferent to our efforts. He wants us to be successful because He loves us and He knows us.

Not making a start is a little like reading, even devouring, many books on prayer until you understand exactly what to do. However, if you never apply that knowledge by doing something about it (i.e. actually praying) you will never experience in reality the things you have read about, they remain theory.

Fred Smith provides a useful useful quote in his book called *Leading with Integrity: Competence With Christian Character*". In his section on "Weighing Character" he says:

> *Character develops when the mind and heart instruct the will in accepting these controlling virtues, out of which come Christlike values and actions.*
>
> **Fred Smith, Weighing Character, in**
> ***Leading with Integrity: Competence With Christian Character***

By applying yourself to the development of your character, you will build your inner strength and confidence. Becoming Christlike in character is more important than the most ecstatic feelings and revelation. Character deals with the heart and so builds power, dignity and integrity.

True character will always reveal itself. Ralph Waldo Emerson once said:

What you are stands over you all the while, and thunders so that I cannot hear you no matter what you say to the contrary.

It is something we may be unaware of and don't think is required so we have to trust in the Holy Spirit to lead us and guide us because we ourselves may be an unsafe barometer of what we are.

The important issue for us is to stay teachable. Make sure you don't believe you are not vulnerable when it comes to any of these points. We all have weak points and it is important to know them. If we were to stay quiet and honest for a moment we, most certainly, would admit what they are and that they have probably been highlighted through the course of this discussion.

I suggest two things that may help. The first is to go before the Holy Spirit and ask Him to show you those areas to work on. I have always found that He will do so. In taking that step the Lord honours that heart and He is willing to work through things with you until you get victory. You may fail miserably in any attempt to grow, but I have always found that being honest with yourself goes a long way. Many years ago I learnt that when I miss it, as I do frequently, that is the time to run to God and not from Him. Repentance is a powerful weapon as I mentioned earlier.

The second is to seek wise counsel and help from a trusted person, or persons, who will walk with you in your endeavours. The idea of a mentor or coach has, perhaps, been overdone in recent years but it is still valid. Ultimately, we have to go beyond protecting our image as others see us and get down to reality. Our true self is our private self that too few see. Jesus is not bothered about our image, He is interested in our worth to Him.

In pursuing this line, sincere confession is a key element that will really help us win. King David provides an example in the passage of scripture when he was faced with the reality that he had made sure Uriah the Hittite was killed in battle so that he could cover up an illicit relationship with Bathsheba. When Nathan the prophet confronted him on this in **2 Samuel 12**. David's response in verse 13 is a valuable lesson for us. Instead of squirming around and making excuses he comes right out from the heart and says:

> *So David said to Nathan "I have sinned against the Lord". And Nathan said to David, "the Lord also has put away your sin; you shall not die...."*

2 Samuel 12:13

Even though he had many faults, his true character came through. It is what makes us stand when we want to run. David accepted the wise counsel of Nathan and changed his ways.

I saw another clear example providing a reason for persevering with building character when my own pastor shared about an experience he had with his brother on a Californian beach. They were surrounded by Navy Seals in training, in what they called "hell week". The reason for that terminology was because the men had to go through some gruelling experiences and they were not allowed to sleep for a week. It is possible to "google" and see images and get information exactly what it entails. I am sure there is a similar program for the British SAS. In essence such action is intended to build character that will stand up under fire.

This is no different to the place we are aiming for in building godly character. Taking steps to change is building credibility in us. That is what God is finally interested in and we can come through to victory. Paul described it well.

> *Therefore I run thus: not with uncertainty. Thus I fight: not as one who beats the air. But I discipline my body and bring it into subjection, lest, when I have preached to others, I myself should become disqualified.*
>
> **1 Corinthians 9:26-27**

So, it is wise to regularly ask ourselves questions like: Am I growing in Christ? Do I want to change? How deep is my desire to walk in holiness and become Christlike?

These are fundamental questions where we reflect on our life and then take action where we see there is a need for change. In doing so we begin to manage our personal life and then this helps us when we relate to others. Why? Because we will demonstrate those soft skills, which we often cannot see but others will, such as humility, courtesy, patience and self control, to name a few.

Finally, I would like to leave you with a couple of important scriptures.

> *...and having done all, to stand. Stand therefore...*
>
> **Ephesians 6:13-14**

This is an encouraging, yet challenging, statement by Paul. It's a point at which he states, at the end of everything he has shared in the letter, that it is important to be strong. That is exactly what we have to do. Be strong, make a stand, make a start because we will not look back.

> *Not that I have already attained, or am already perfected; but I press on, that I may lay hold of that for which Christ Jesus laid hold of me. Brethren, I do not count myself to have apprehended: but one thing I do, forgetting those things which are behind and reaching forward to those things which are ahead, I press forward toward the goal for the prize of the upward call of God in Christ Jesus.*
>
> **Philippians 3:12-14**

In conclusion, a clear observation is that none of us have made it and none of us are perfect, something Paul recognised acutely even though he achieved so much in his life. However, Paul also recognised the importance of not looking back and thinking about what could have been or what should have been. Instead, he determined at all times to keep pressing forward.

So let me encourage us all to do the same. It is possible to begin to develop a better godly character than we have now. We just have to step forward and do it. I am convinced Holy Spirit will back you all the way and so will other people when they see a change happening in front of them. It's worth the effort so let's do it.

About the Author

Tony Sheard is an accomplished and passionate speaker with a heart to bring fresh purpose and direction in the Christian world today and, especially, to help build the local church and transform lives to be all that God has for them.

Tony was born in Yorkshire and, with his wife Julie, currently lives just outside Bath in the UK.

Having spent a number of years as a speaker in various churches throughout Europe and the USA, Tony and Julie became the first European Directors of Jesse Duplantis Ministries, steering the office successfully through 5 years of pioneer growth.

During this time they received a call from God to Pastor and formed Living Word Christian Centre, which they led together for 9 years. Tony longs to see people fulfil the destiny and purpose on their lives. He is determined to see the Holy Spirit move powerfully as signs follow the preaching of the Word.

On the prompting of the Lord, he stepped out of Pastoring and formed Living Word UK as an outreach of LWCC in order to carry this message to the world. That is, together with a compassion to support those who need help, which is a vital part of the ministry. Tony has a heart to come alongside churches and work with them as they fulfil the vision of God in their communities.

Tony is chair of Trustees of Kenneth Copeland Ministries Europe, council member of Churches in Community International and has developed coaching skills working one on one with ministers. He regularly supports pastors with strategic planning and helps ministry training.

Printed in Great Britain
by Amazon

47772170R00059